EASY PIANO

# BROADWAY SONGS FOR KIDS

## 2ND EDITION

ISBN 978-1-4950-8569-7

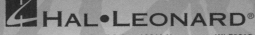

7777 W. BLUEMOUND RD. P.O. BOX 13819 MILWAUKEE, WI 53213

Visit Hal Leonard Online at
www.halleonard.com

# CONTENTS

# BEAUTY AND THE BEAST
from BEAUTY AND THE BEAST: THE BROADWAY MUSICAL

Music by ALAN MENKEN
Lyrics by HOWARD ASHMAN

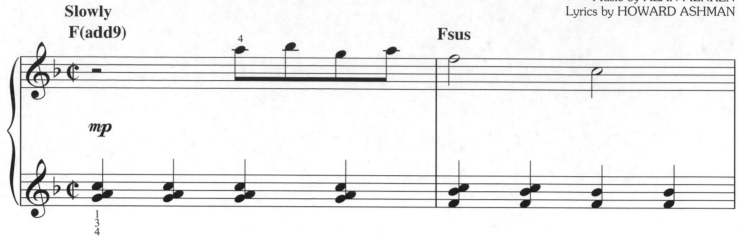

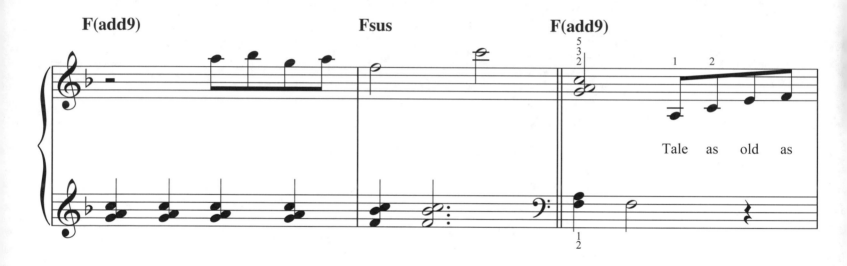

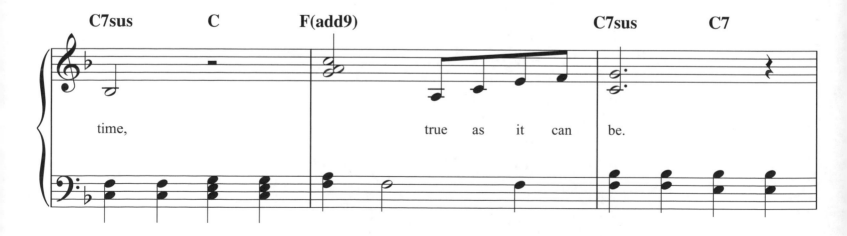

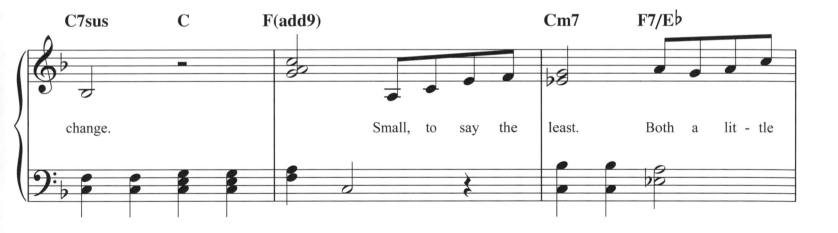

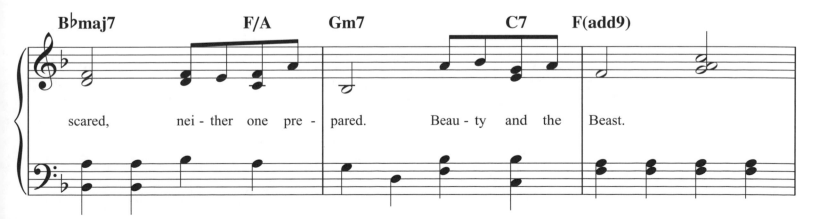

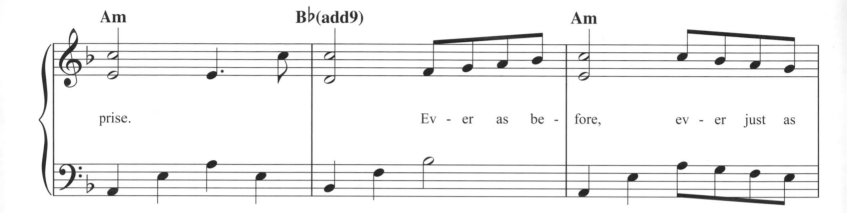

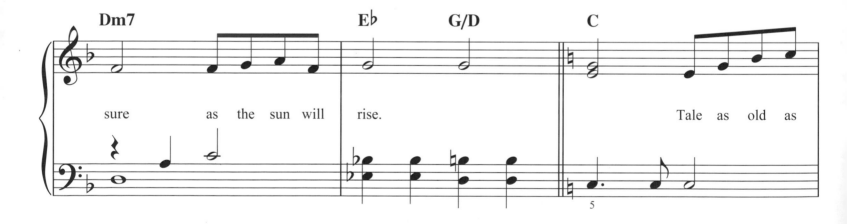

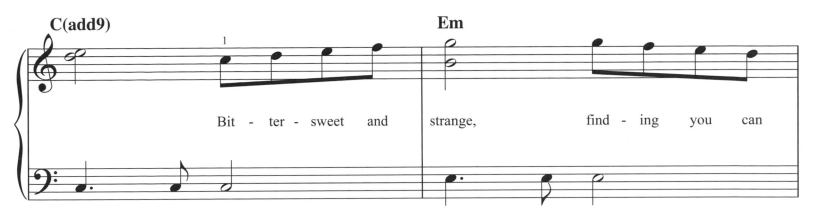

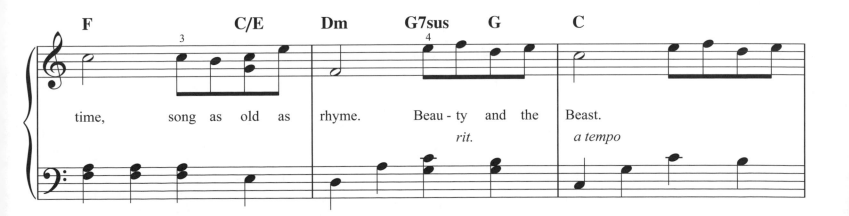

Tale    as    old    as    time,        song    as    old    as

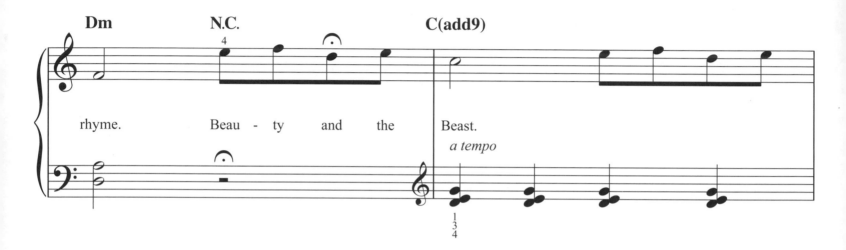

rhyme.        Beau - ty    and    the        Beast.

*a tempo*

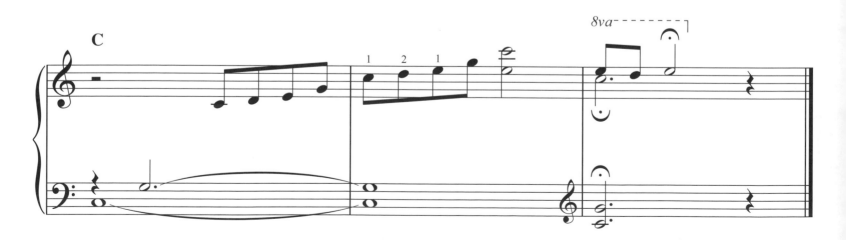

# CASTLE ON A CLOUD
## from LES MISÉRABLES

Music by CLAUDE-MICHEL SCHÖNBERG
Lyrics by ALAIN BOUBLIL, JEAN-MARC NATEL
and HERBERT KRETZMER

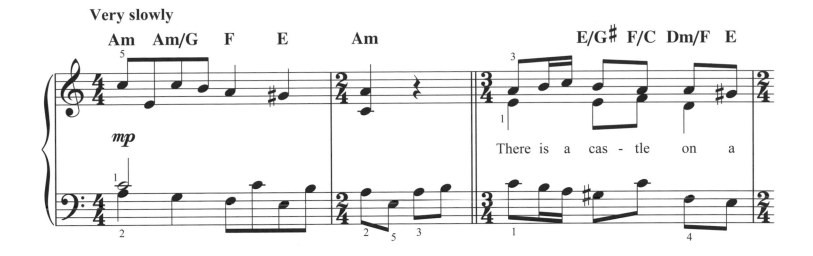

nice to see and she's soft to touch. She says, "Co - sette, I love you ver - y much."

I know a place where no one's lost.

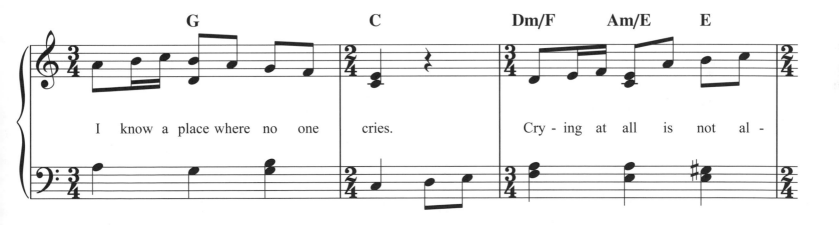

I know a place where no one cries. Cry - ing at all is not al -

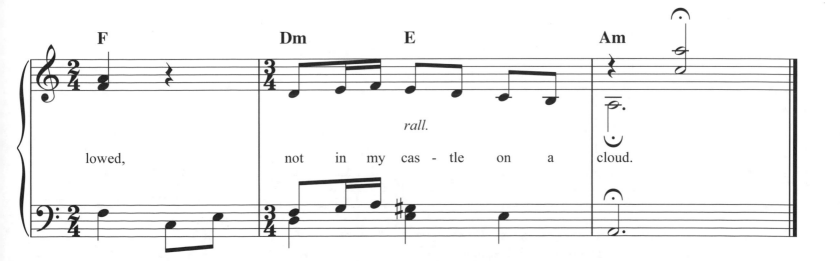

lowed, not in my cas - tle on a cloud.

# DO-RE-MI
## from THE SOUND OF MUSIC

Lyrics by OSCAR HAMMERSTEIN II
Music by RICHARD RODGERS

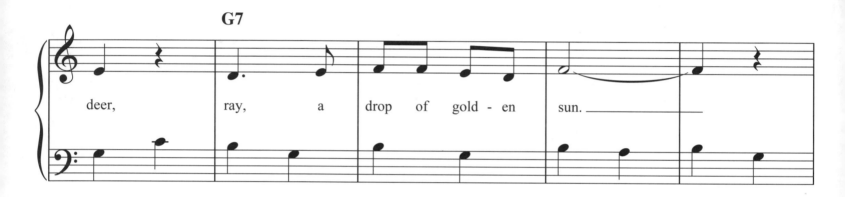

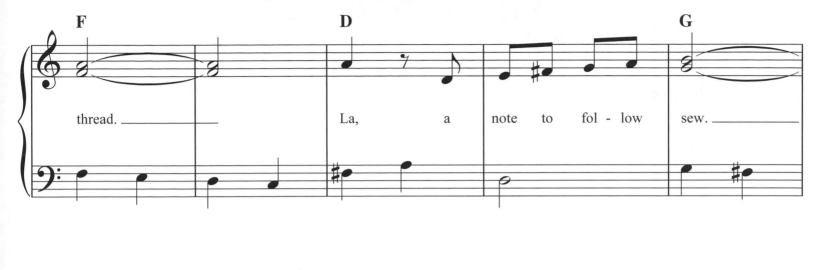

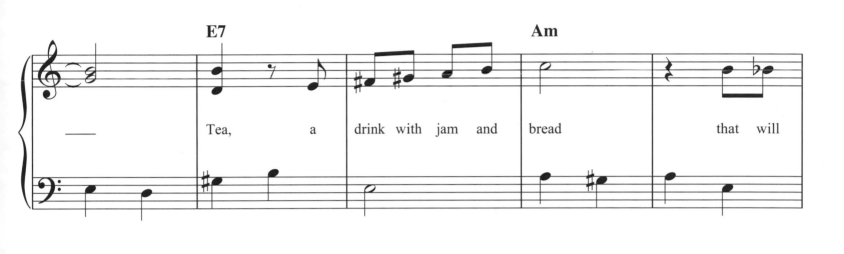

# GARY, INDIANA
### from Meredith Willson's THE MUSIC MAN

By MEREDITH WILLSON

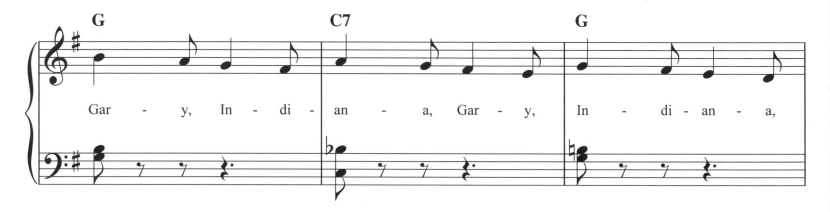

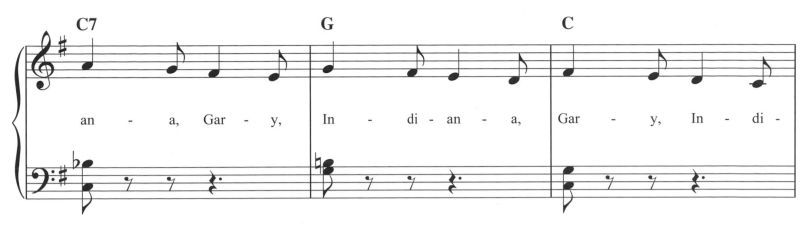

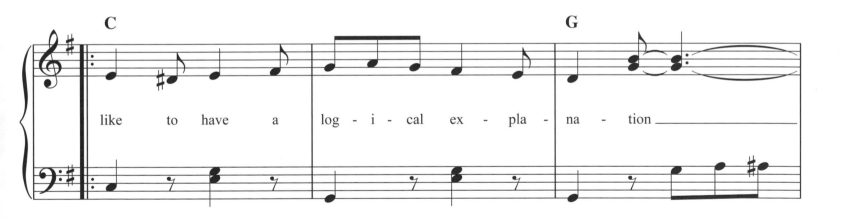

I will say with-out a mo-ment of hes-i-ta-tion, ___

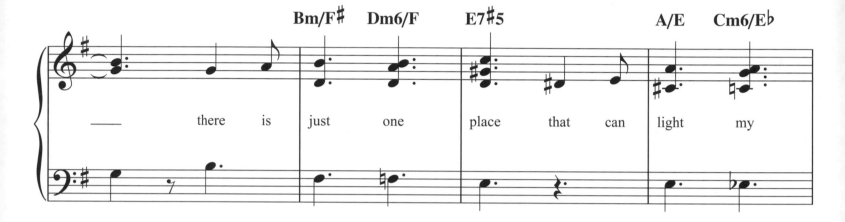

**Bm/F♯**  **Dm6/F**  **E7♯5**  **A/E**  **Cm6/E♭**

___ there is just one place that can light my

**D7♯5**  **G**  **C7**

face. Gar - y, In - di - an - a, Gar - y,

**G**  **C**  **G**

In - di - an - a, not Lou - is - i - an - a, Par - is,

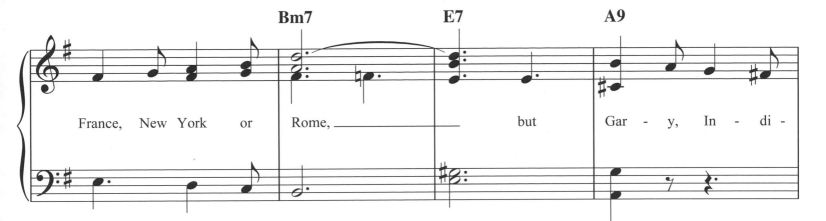

France, New York or Rome, _____ but Gar - y, In - di -

an - a, Gar - y, In - di - an - a, Gar - y, In - di -

an - a, my home, sweet home. _____ If you'd

home.

# I KNOW IT'S TODAY
## from SHREK THE MUSICAL

Words and Music by DAVID LINDSAY-ABAIRE
and JEANINE TESORI

**Moderately fast**

There's a prin-cess in a tow-er. Oh, my gosh, that's

just like me. Poor Ra-pun-zel needs a hair-cut,

but the witch won't set her free. She pass-es time by sing-ing, like

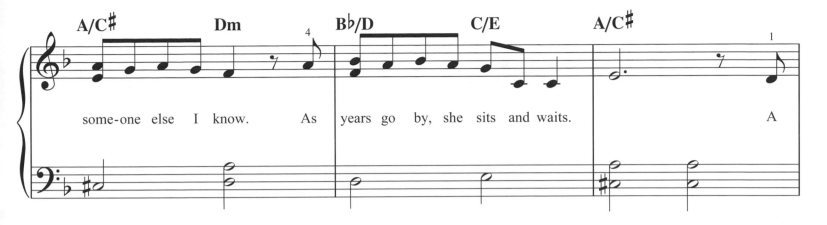

some-one else I know. As years go by, she sits and waits. A

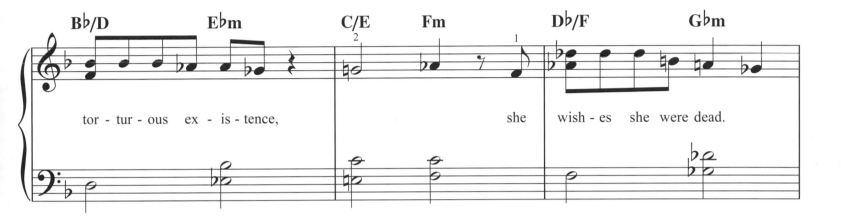

tor - tur - ous ex - is - tence, she wish - es she were dead.

But in the end, Ra - pun - zel finds a mil - lion-aire. The

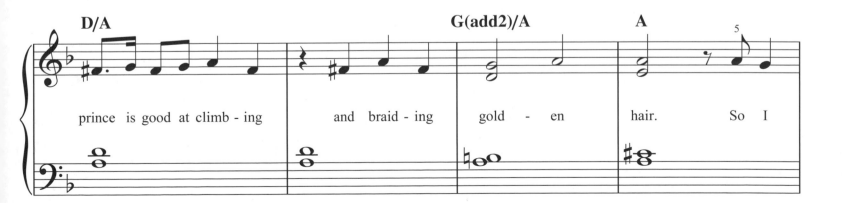

prince is good at climb - ing and braid - ing gold - en hair. So I

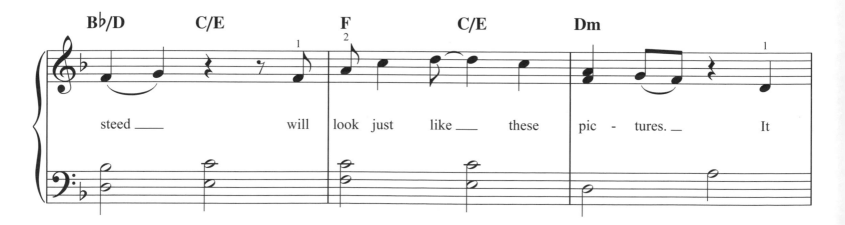

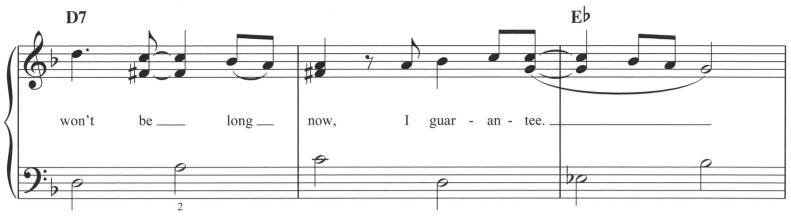

won't be \_\_\_ long \_\_\_ now, I guar - an - tee. \_\_\_

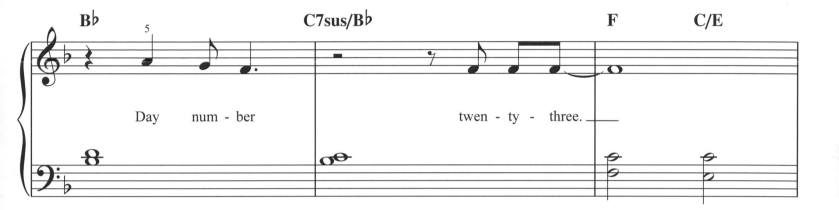

Day num - ber twen - ty - three. \_\_\_

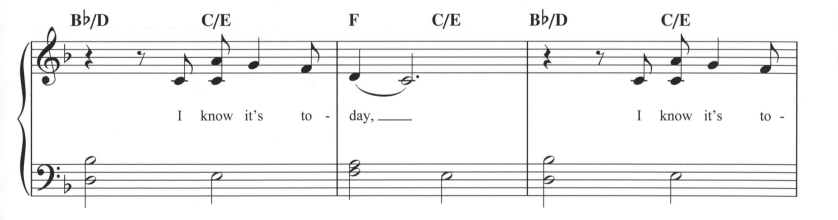

I know it's to - day, \_\_\_ I know it's to -

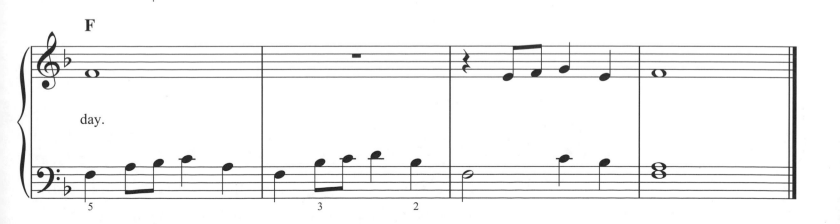

day.

# I WHISTLE A HAPPY TUNE

## from THE KING AND I

Lyrics by OSCAR HAMMERSTEIN II
Music by RICHARD RODGERS

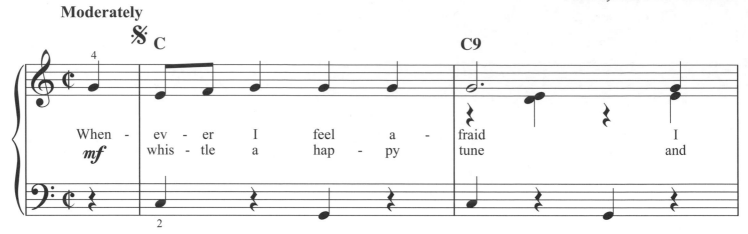

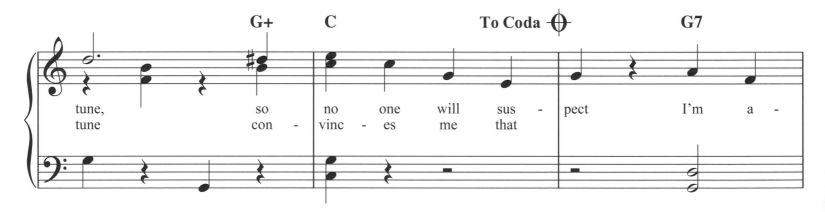

strike a care - less pose and whis - tle a hap - py

tune and no one ev - er knows I'm a - fraid. _____

_____ The re - sult of this de - cep - tion is

ver - y strange to _____ tell, for when I fool the

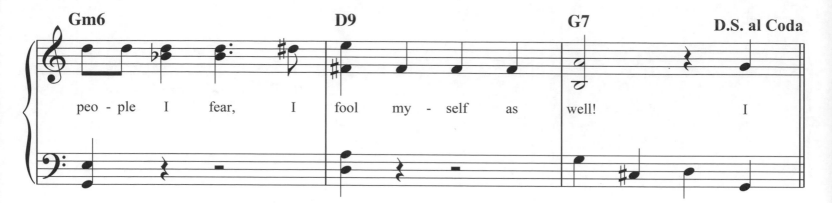

**Gm6**  **D9**  **G7**  **D.S. al Coda**

peo - ple I fear, I fool my - self as well! I

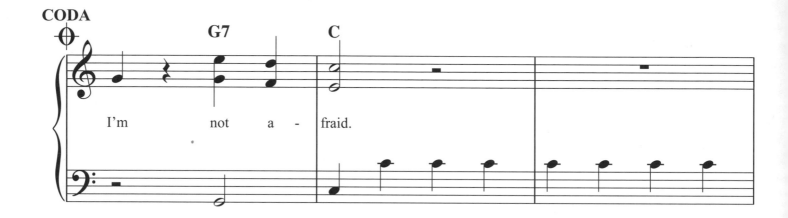

**CODA**  **G7**  **C**

I'm not a - fraid.

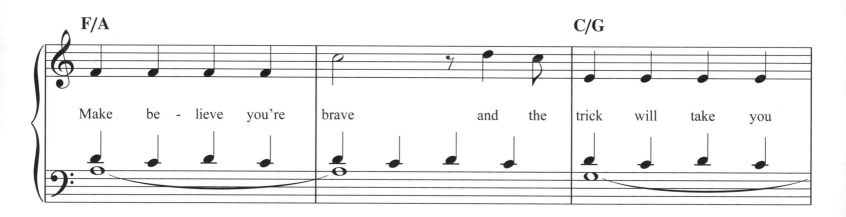

**F/A**  **C/G**

Make be - lieve you're brave and the trick will take you

**F/A**

far. You may be as brave as you

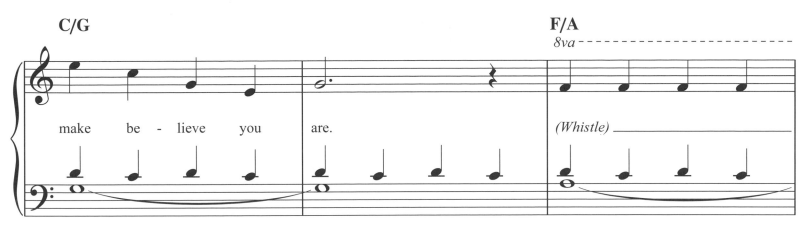

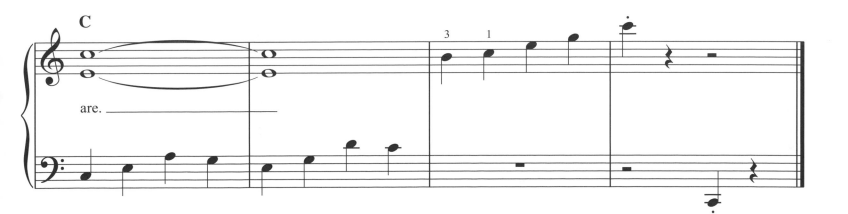

where and the world will o-pen its arms to

me. I'm a young Nor - we - gian

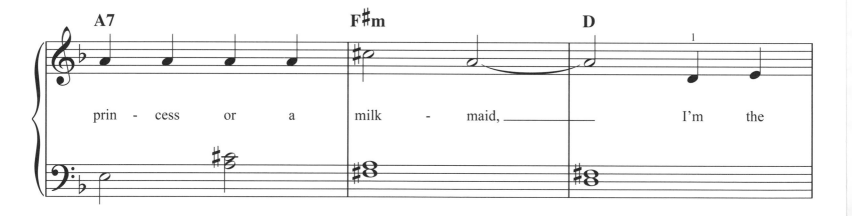

prin - cess or a milk - maid, I'm the

great - est pri - ma don - na in Mi - lan.

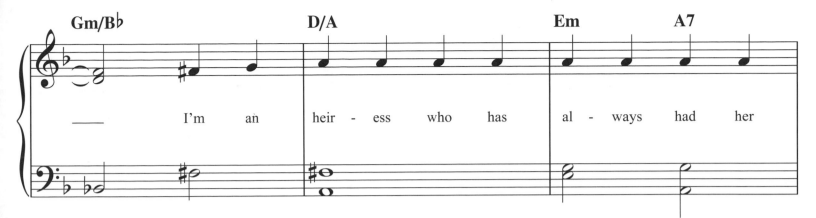

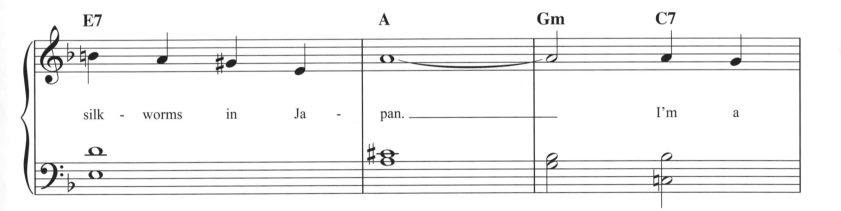

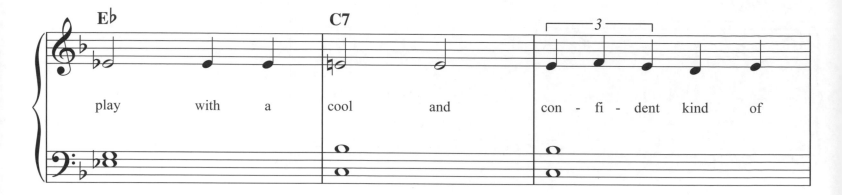

play with a cool and con - fi - dent kind of

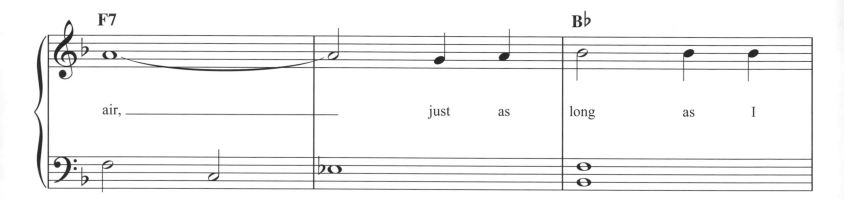

air, _____ just as long as I

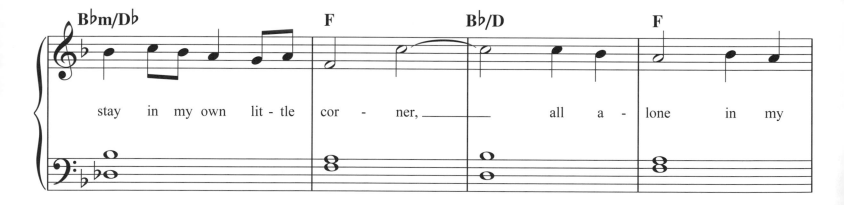

stay in my own lit - tle cor - ner, \_\_\_\_\_ all a - lone in my

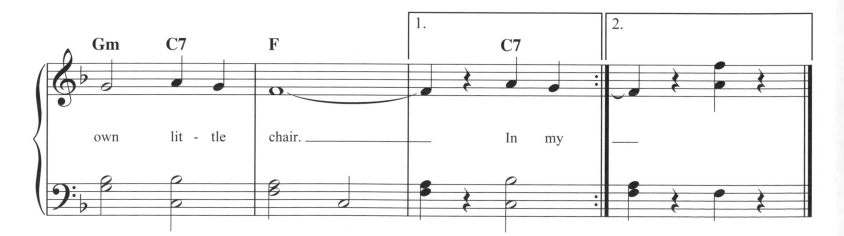

own lit - tle chair. \_\_\_\_\_ In my

# LITTLE PEOPLE
## from LES MISÉRABLES

Music by CLAUDE-MICHEL SCHÖNBERG
Lyrics by ALAIN BOUBLIL,
JEAN-MARC NATEL and HERBERT KRETZMER

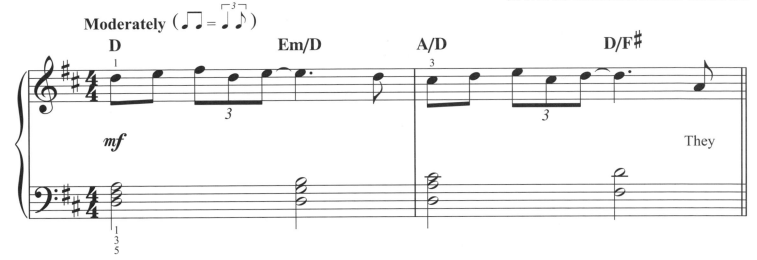

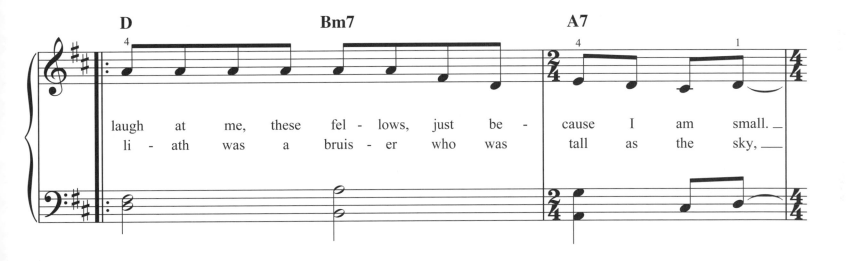

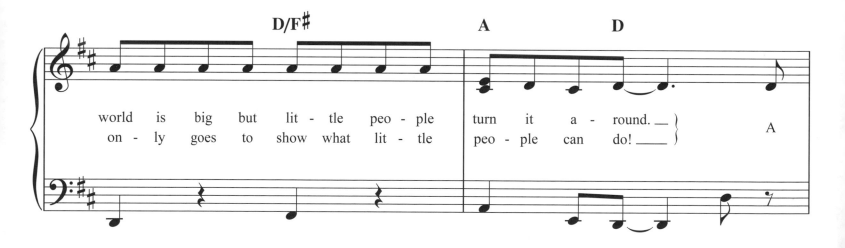

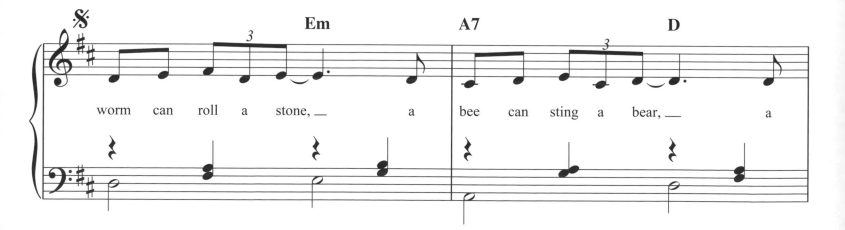

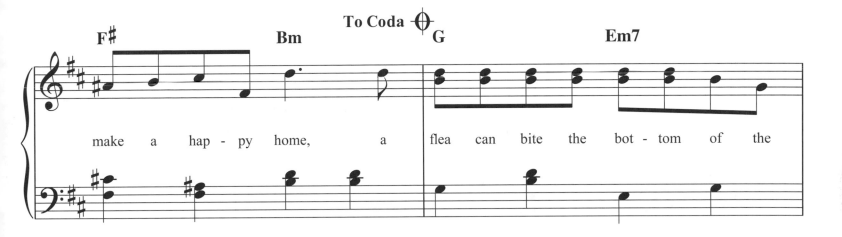

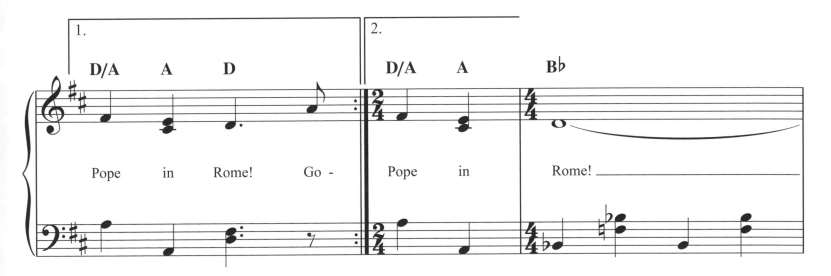

head in the cloud. _____ It's of - ten kind of use - ful to get

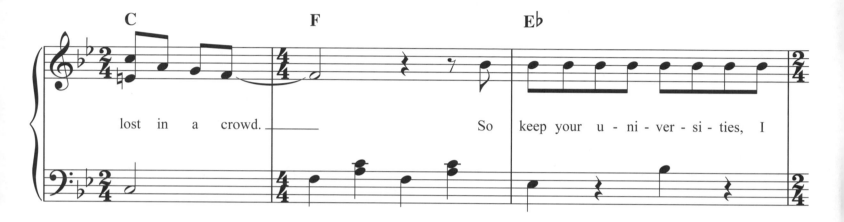

lost in a crowd. _____ So keep your u - ni - ver - si - ties, I

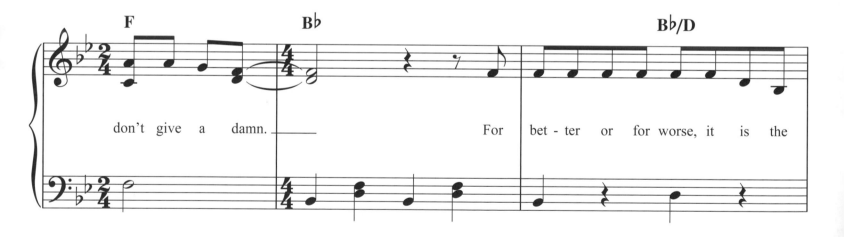

don't give a damn. _____ For bet - ter or for worse, it is the

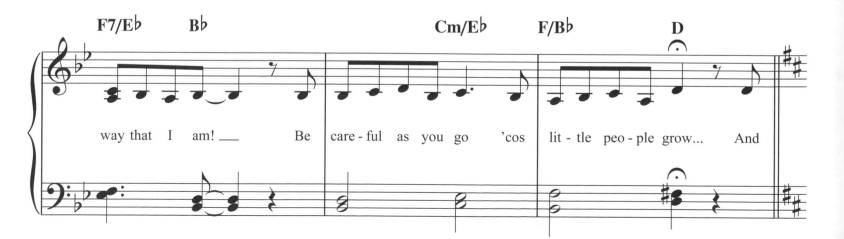

way that I am! ___ Be care - ful as you go 'cos lit - tle peo - ple grow... And

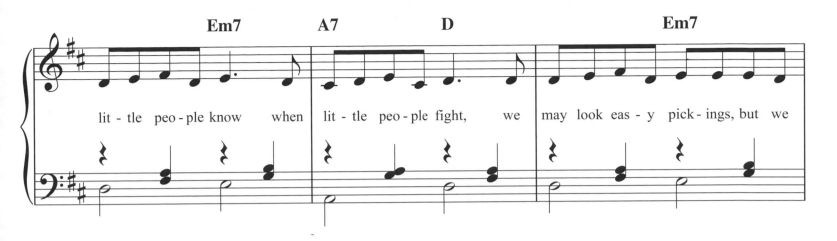

lit - tle peo - ple know when lit - tle peo - ple fight, we may look eas - y pick - ings, but we

got some bite! So nev - er kick a dog be - cause it's just a pup. You

bet - ter run for cov - er when the pup grows up! And we'll fight like twen - ty ar - mies and we

**D.S. al Coda**

won't give up! A

**CODA**

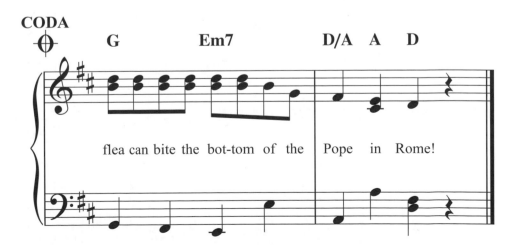

flea can bite the bot - tom of the Pope in Rome!

# INTO THE WOODS

**from INTO THE WOODS**
**Film Version**

Music and Lyrics by
STEPHEN SONDHEIM

**Alla marcia, leggiero, jauntily**

In - to the woods, it's time to go. I hate to leave, I have to, though.

In - to the woods—it's time, and so I must be - gin my jour - ney.

Into the woods, and through the trees To where I am ex-pect-ed, ma'am.

Into the woods to Grand-moth-er's house...

Into the woods to Grand-moth-er's house...

The
sub. **p**

*sempre staccato*

way is clear, The light is good, I have no fear, Nor

no one should. The woods are just trees, The trees are just wood. I

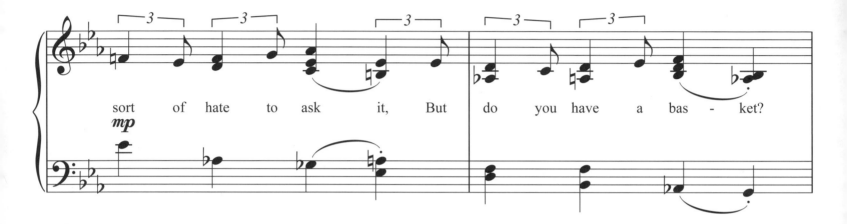

sort of hate to ask it, But do you have a bas - ket?

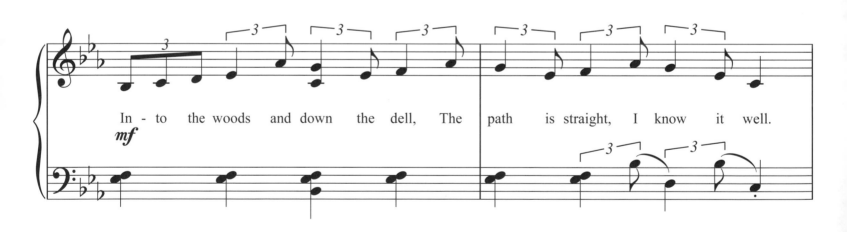

In - to the woods and down the dell, The path is straight, I know it well.

In - to the woods, and who can tell What's wait - ing on the jour - ney?

# IT'S THE HARD-KNOCK LIFE

## from the Musical Production ANNIE

Lyric by MARTIN CHARNIN
Music by CHARLES STROUSE

**Quickly, with a tough edge**

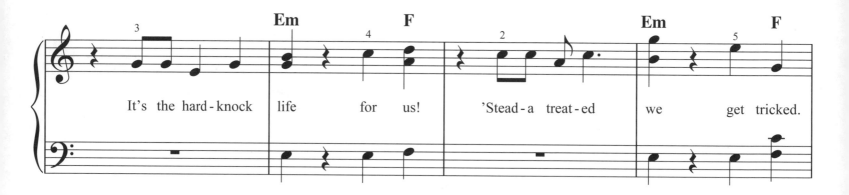

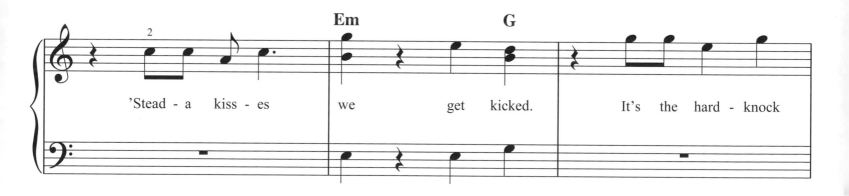

row we hoe. Cot - ton blan - kets 'stead - a wool, __

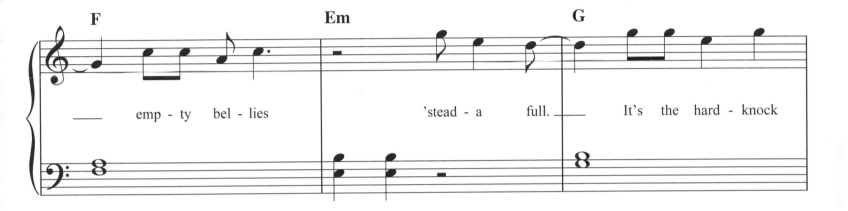

__ emp - ty bel - lies 'stead - a full. __ It's the hard - knock

life. Don't it feel like the wind is al - ways

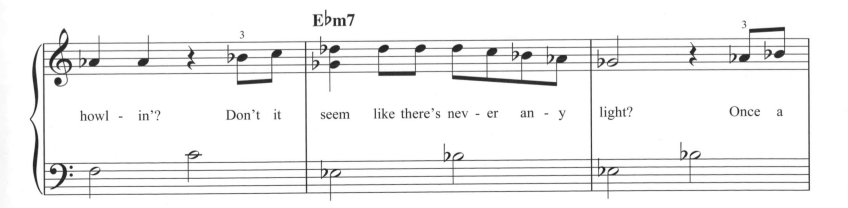

howl - in'? Don't it seem like there's nev - er an - y light? Once a

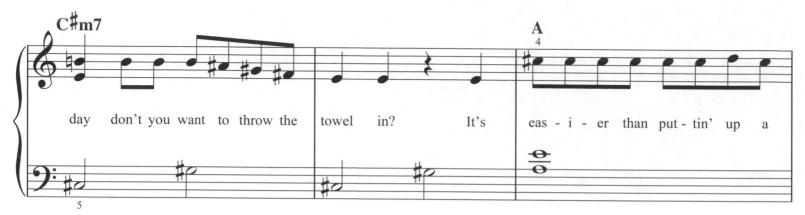

day  don't you want  to throw the    towel   in?        It's      eas - i - er  than  put - tin'  up  a

fight.            No one's   there   when your dreams at  night get     creep - y.            No one

cares    if    you   grow   or   if   you     shrink.                    No    one

dries   when  your   eyes   get   wet  and    weep - y.            From   the

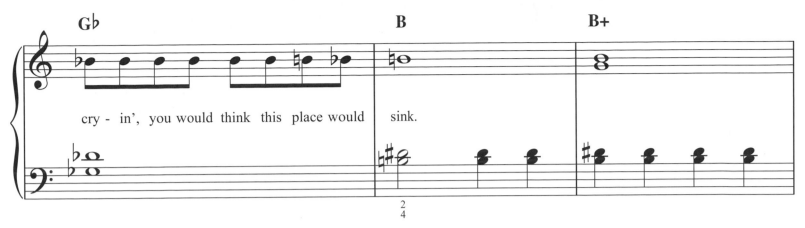

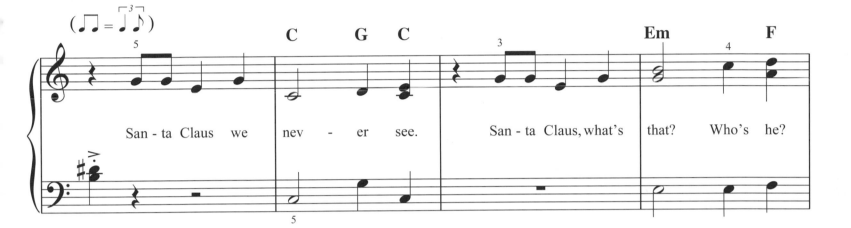

# LET ME ENTERTAIN YOU

## from GYPSY

Lyrics by STEPHEN SONDHEIM
Music by JULE STYNE

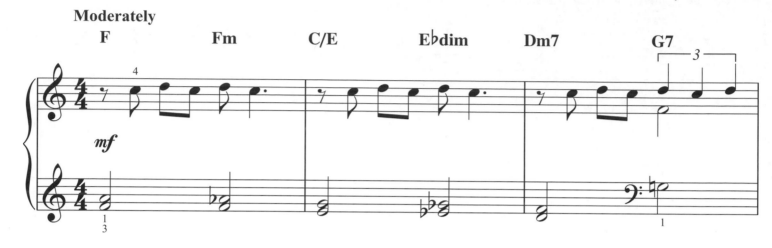

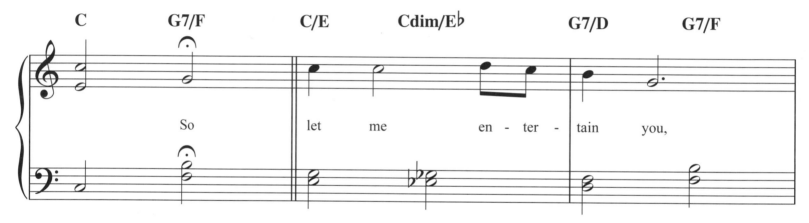

So let me en - ter - tain you,

let me make you smile. Let me do a few tricks, some

old and then some new tricks, I'm ver - y ver - sa -

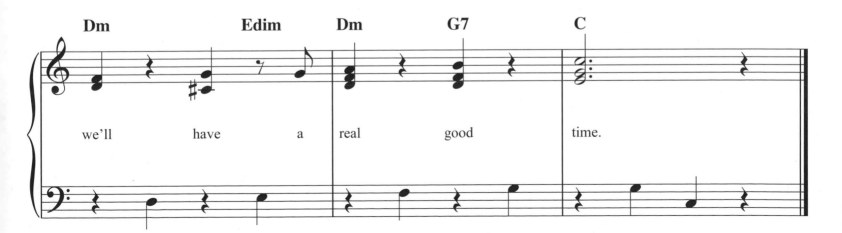

# PART OF YOUR WORLD
## from THE LITTLE MERMAID - A BROADWAY MUSICAL

Music by ALAN MENKEN
Lyrics by HOWARD ASHMAN

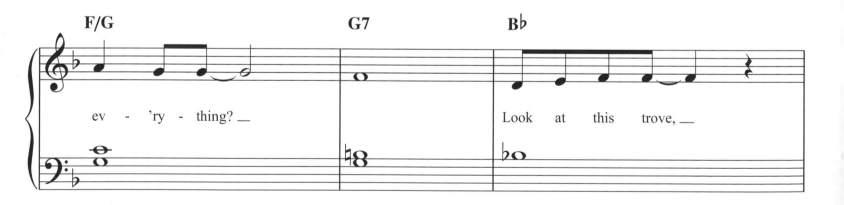

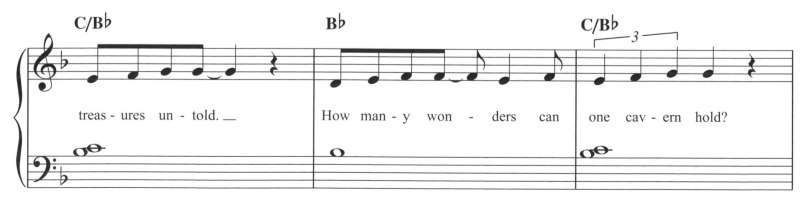

Looking a - round___ here you'd think___ sure, she's got ev - 'ry - thing.___

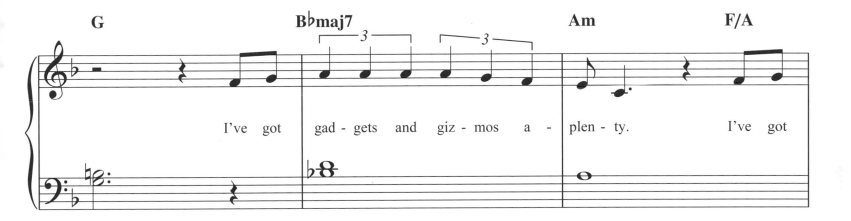

I've got gad - gets and giz - mos a - plen - ty. I've got

who - zits and what - zits ga - lore. You want thing - a - ma - bobs, I've got

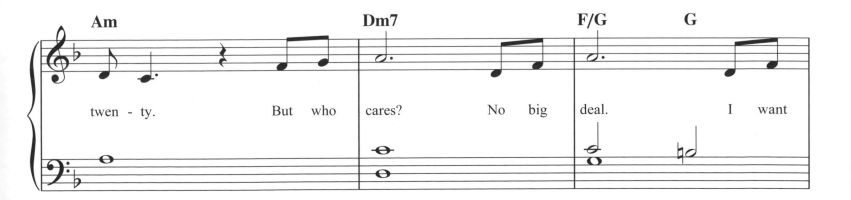

twen - ty. But who cares? No big deal. I want

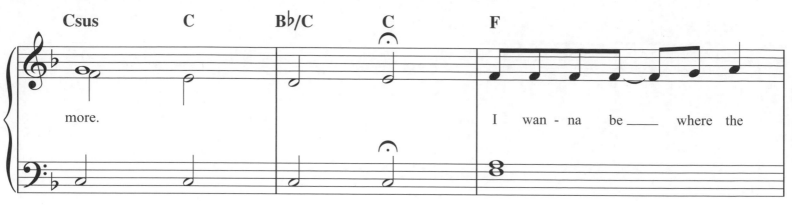

more.

I wan - na be ___ where the

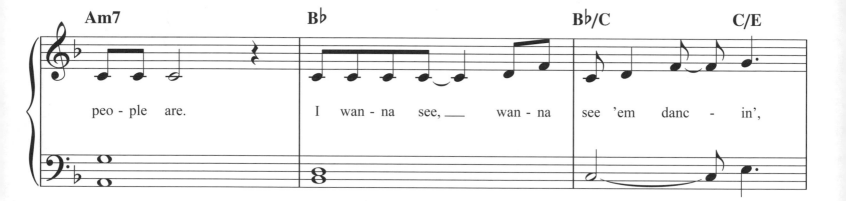

peo - ple are.

I wan - na see, ___ wan - na see 'em danc - in',

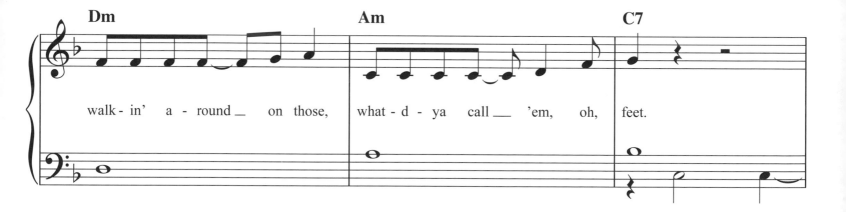

walk - in' a - round ___ on those,

what - d - ya call ___ 'em, oh, feet.

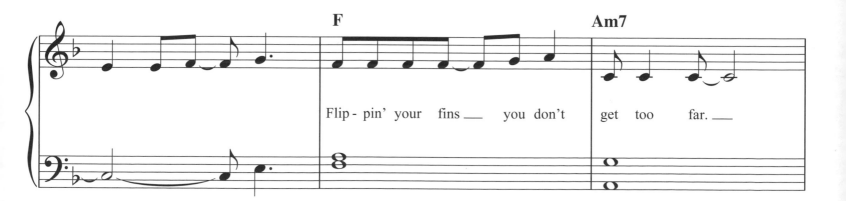

Flip - pin' your fins ___ you don't

get too far. ___

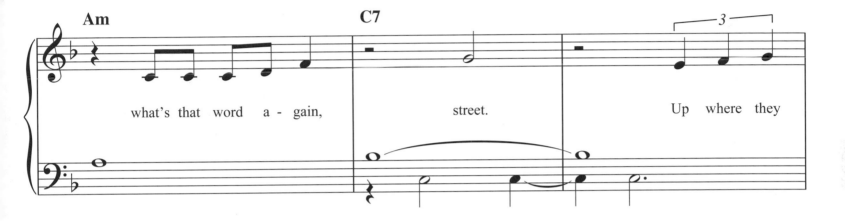

50

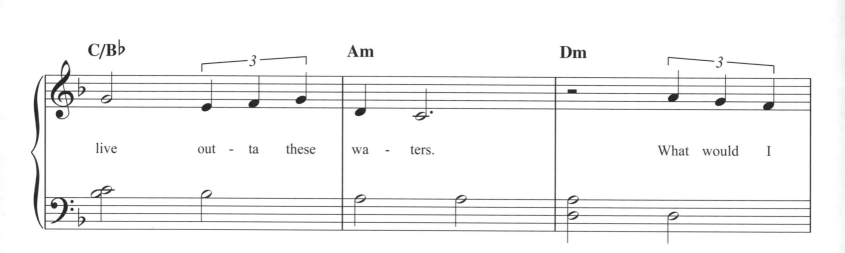

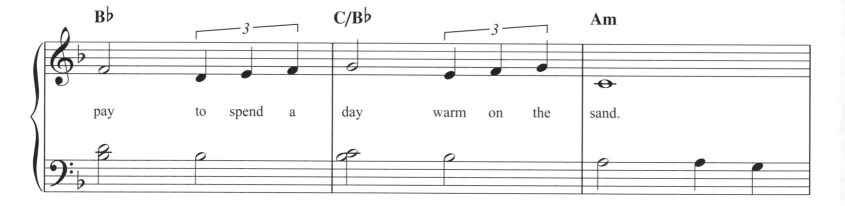

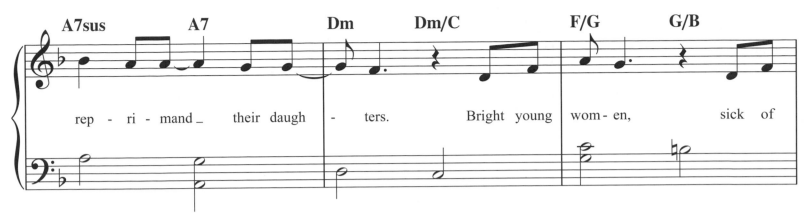

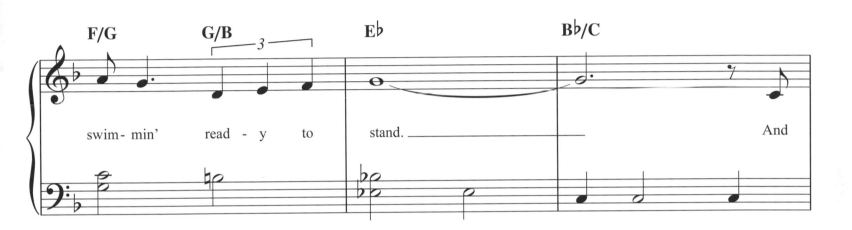

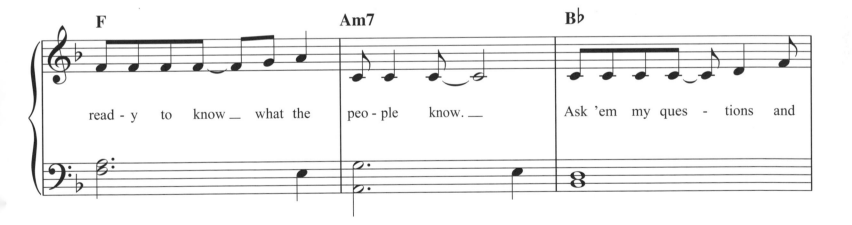

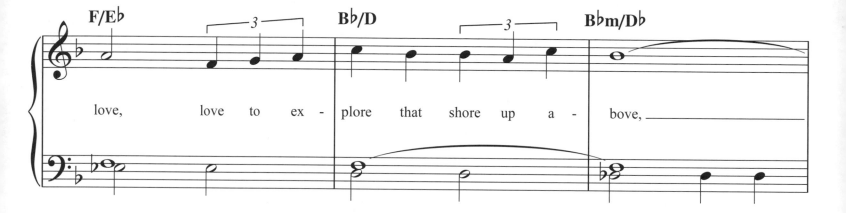

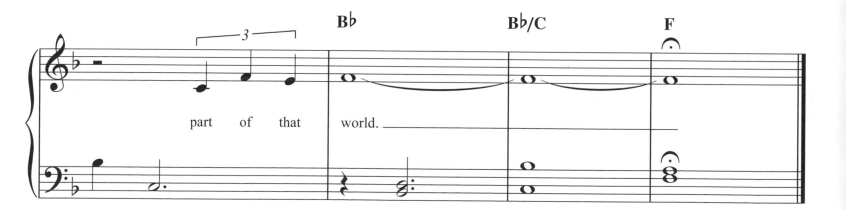

# MAYBE
## from the Musical Production ANNIE

Lyric by MARTIN CHARNIN
Music by CHARLES STROUSE

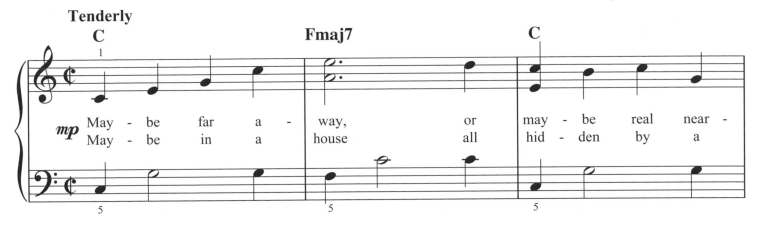

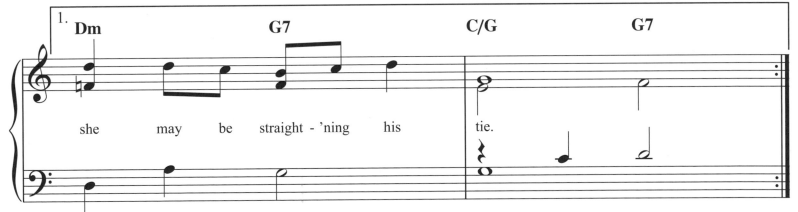

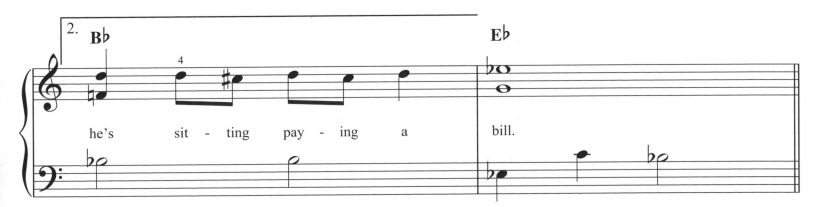

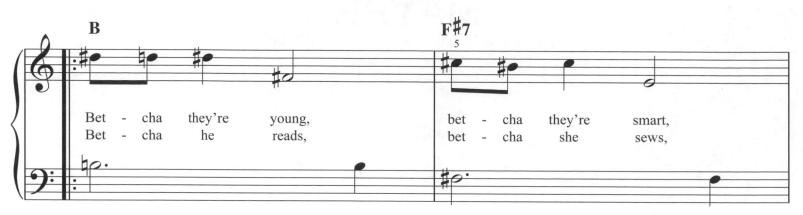

**B**                               **F#7**

Bet - cha they're young,     bet - cha they're smart,
Bet - cha he reads,     bet - cha she sews,

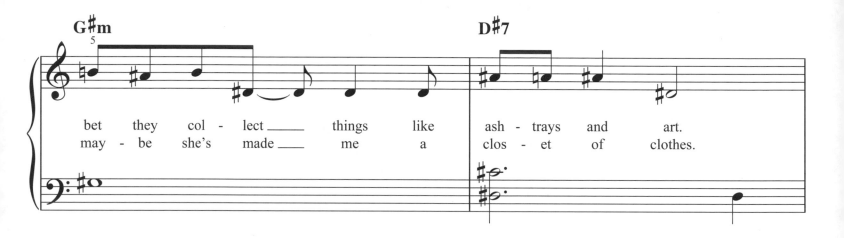

**G#m**                             **D#7**

bet they col - lect ____ things like     ash - trays and art.
may - be she's made ____ me a     clos - et of clothes.

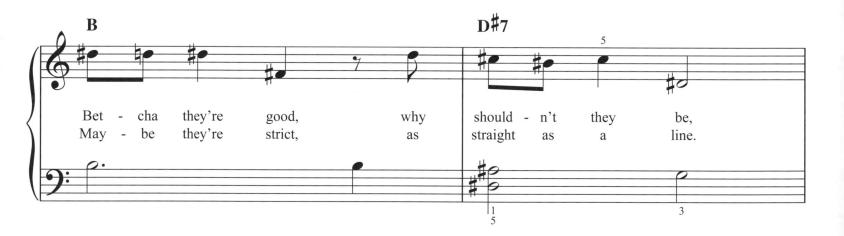

**B**                             **D#7**

Bet - cha they're good,     why should - n't they be,
May - be they're strict,     as straight as a line.

**G#m**                  **G7**

their one mis - take was giv - ing up me.        So,
Don't real - ly care as long as they're mine.       So,

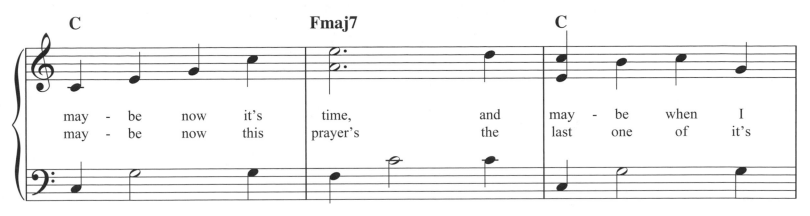

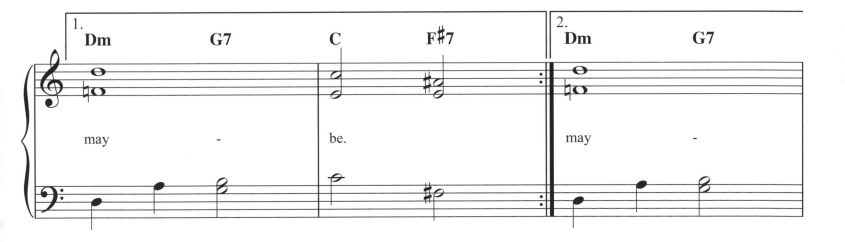

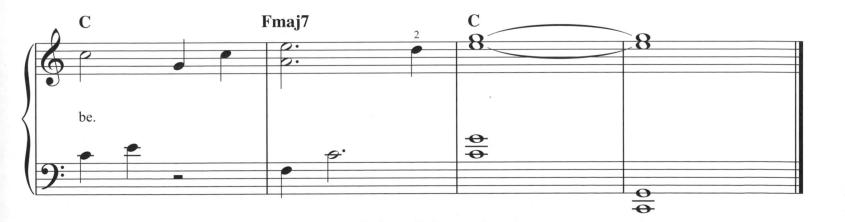

# NAUGHTY
## from MATILDA THE MUSICAL

Words and Music by
TIM MINCHIN

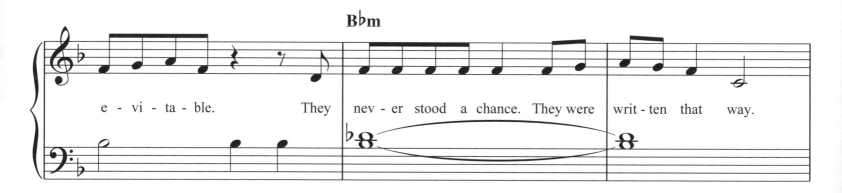

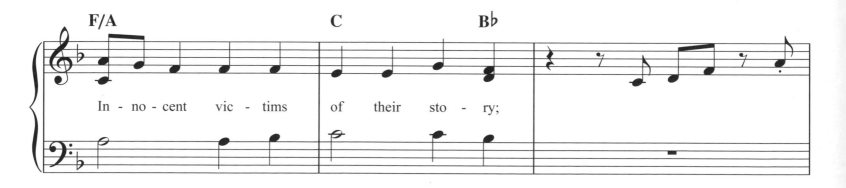

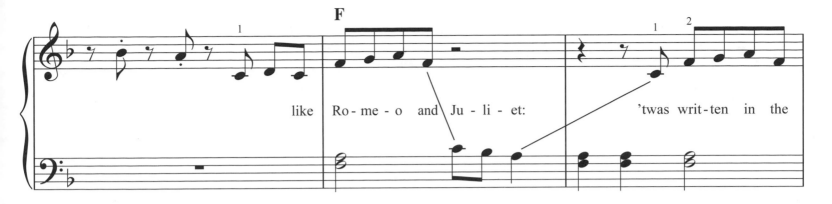

like Ro-me-o and Ju-li-et: 'twas writ-ten in the

stars be-fore they e-ven met that love and fate and a

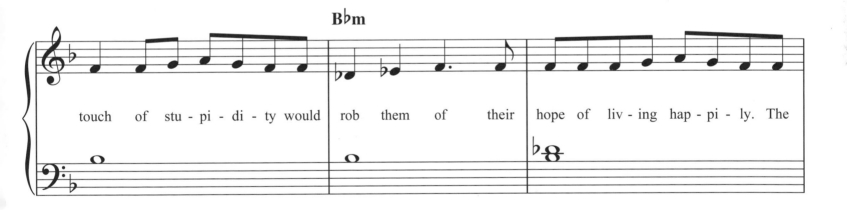

touch of stu-pi-di-ty would rob them of their hope of liv-ing hap-pi-ly. The

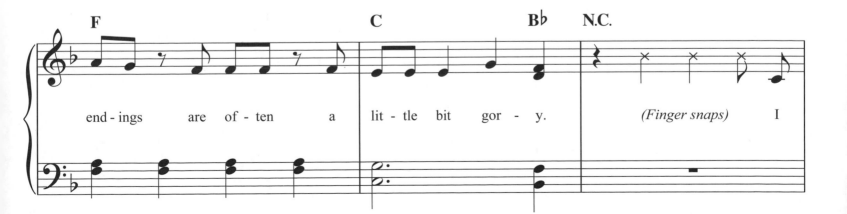

end-ings are of-ten a lit-tle bit gor-y. *(Finger snaps)* I

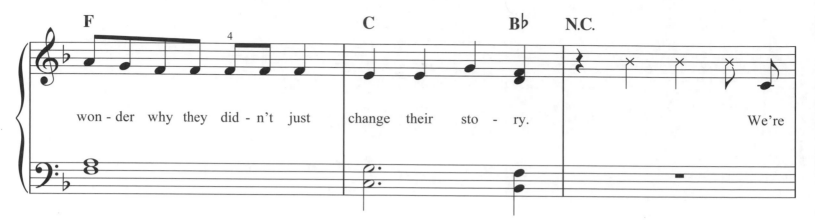

won-der why they did-n't just change their sto-ry. We're

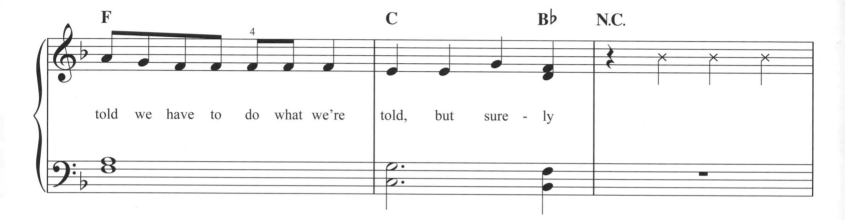

told we have to do what we're told, but sure-ly

some-times you have to be a lit-tle bit naugh-ty.

Just be-cause you find that

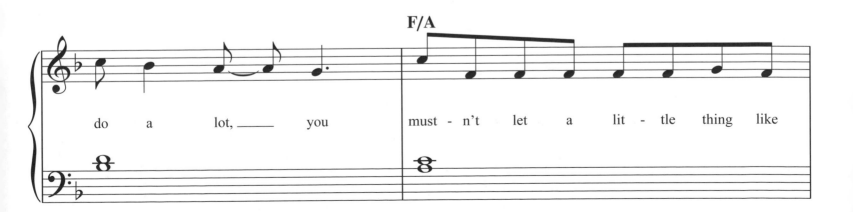

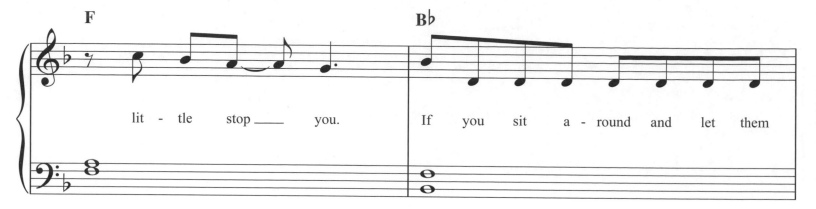

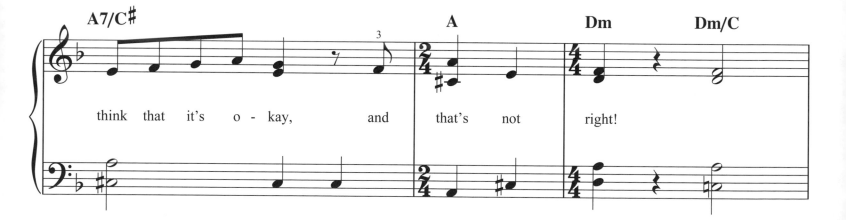

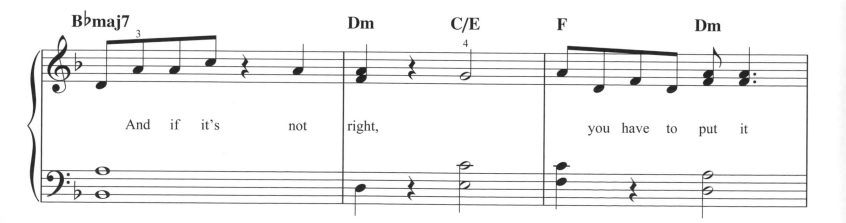

E7

A7

Gm7

right.

But no - bod - y else ___ is gon - na

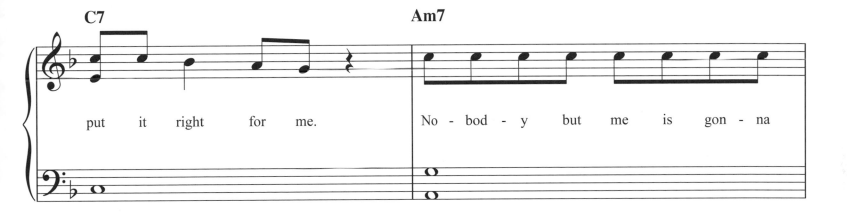

C7

Am7

put it right for me.

No - bod - y but me is gon - na

D7

Gm7/F

change my sto - ry.

Some - times you have to be a

C

F    N.C.

F

lit - tle bit naught - y.

# THE PERFECT NANNY

**from MARY POPPINS**

Words and Music by RICHARD M. SHERMAN
and ROBERT B. SHERMAN

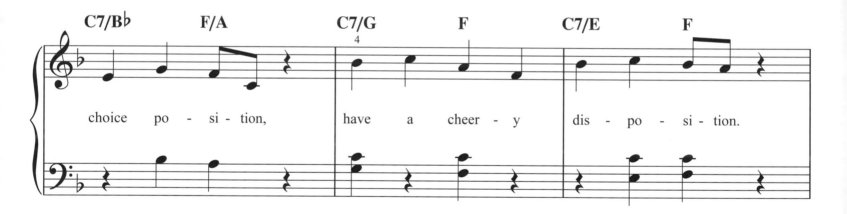

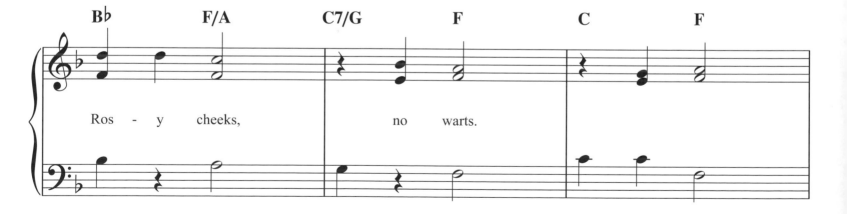

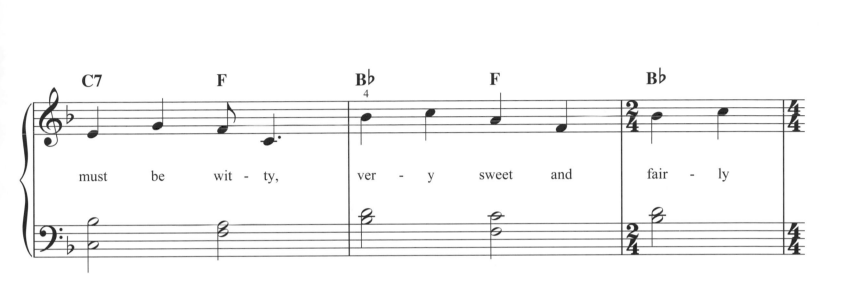

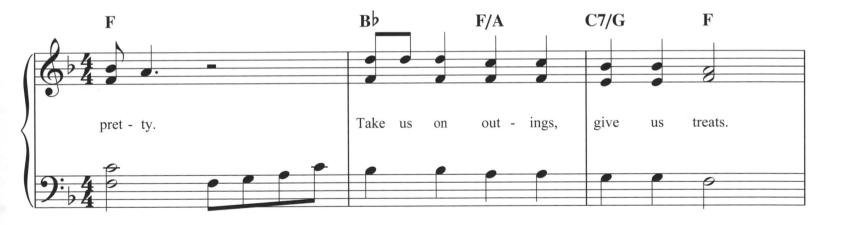

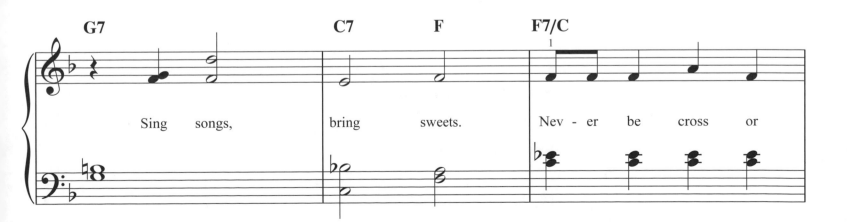

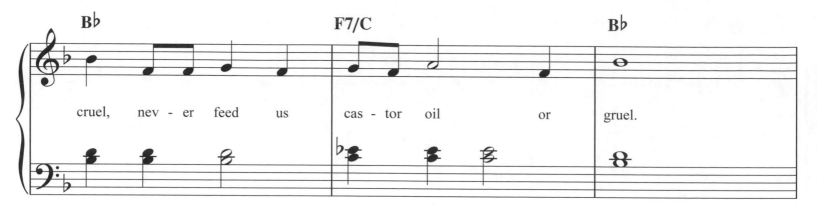

cruel, nev - er feed us cas - tor oil or gruel.

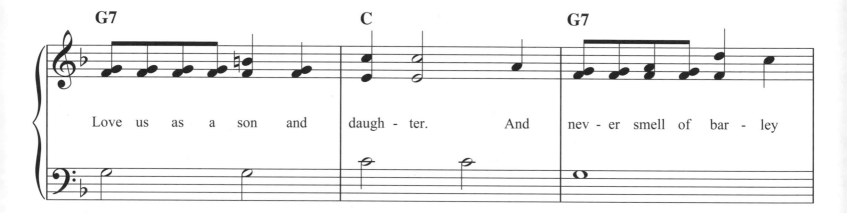

Love us as a son and daugh - ter. And nev - er smell of bar - ley

wa - ter. If you won't scold and

dom - i - nate us, we will nev - er give you cause to

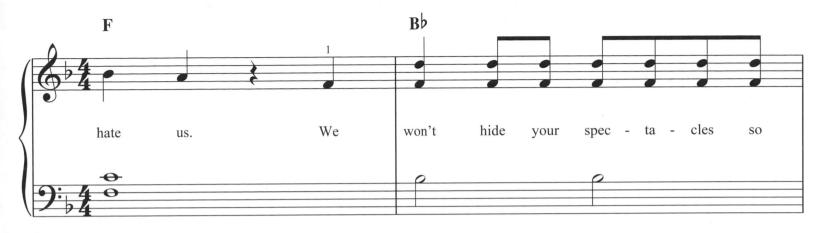

hate us. We won't hide your spec - ta - cles so

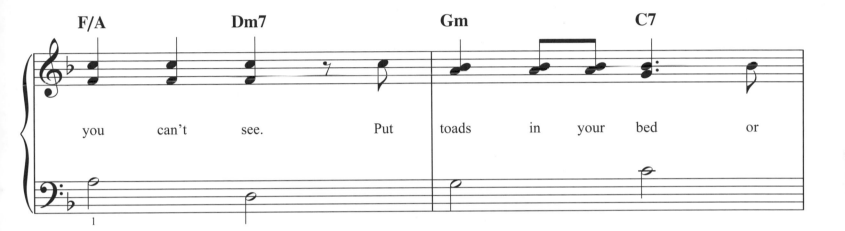

you can't see. Put toads in your bed or

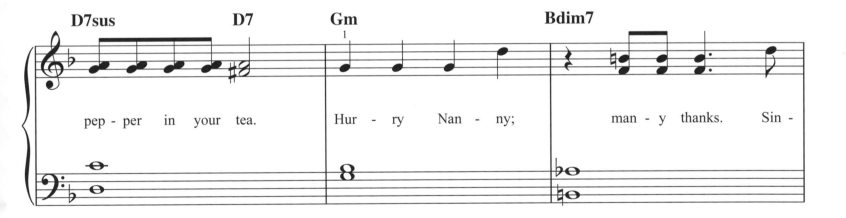

pep - per in your tea. Hur - ry Nan - ny; man - y thanks. Sin -

cere - ly, Jane and Mi - chael Banks.

# THE SOUND OF MUSIC
## from THE SOUND OF MUSIC

Lyrics by OSCAR HAMMERSTEIN II
Music by RICHARD RODGERS

**Moderately fast**

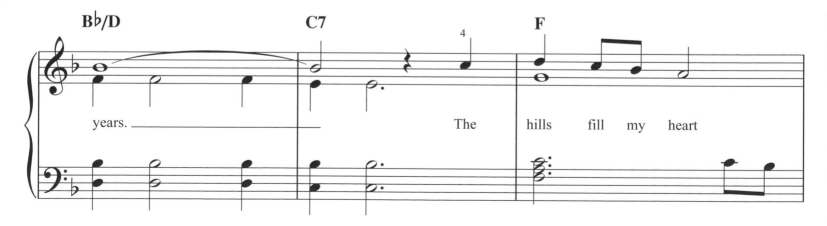

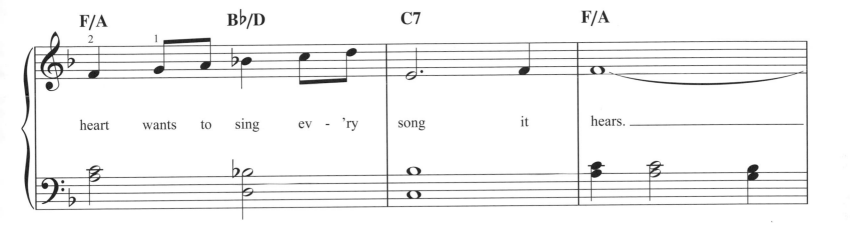

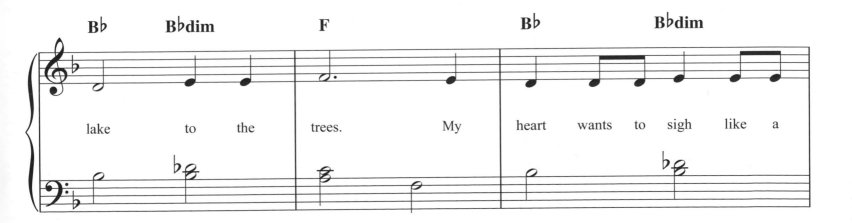

chime that flies from a church on a breeze, to laugh like a brook when it

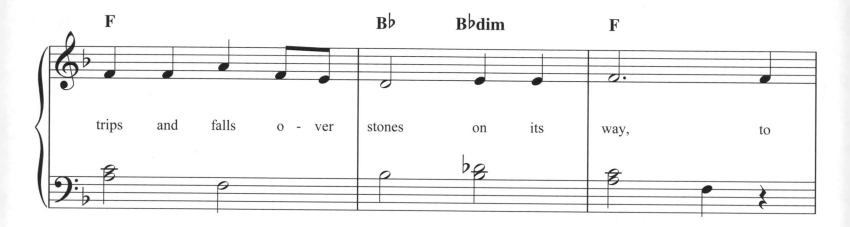

trips and falls o - ver stones on its way, to

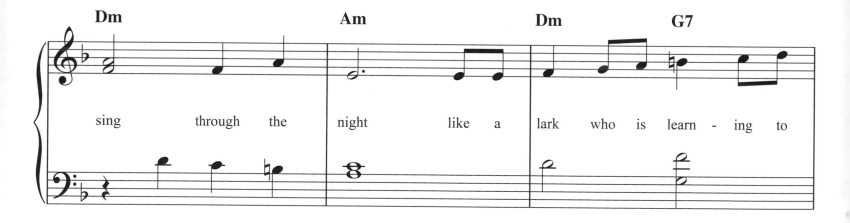

sing through the night like a lark who is learn - ing to

pray. I go to the hills when my heart is

lone - ly, _____ I know I will hear what I've heard be -

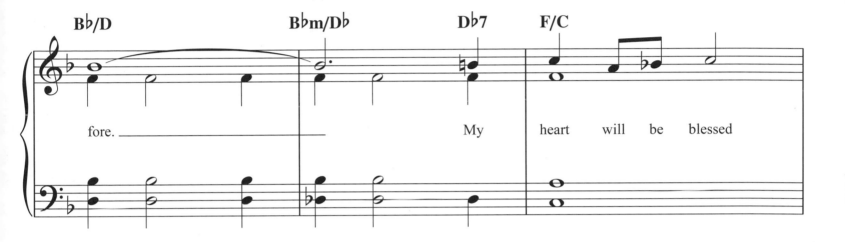

fore. _____ My heart will be blessed

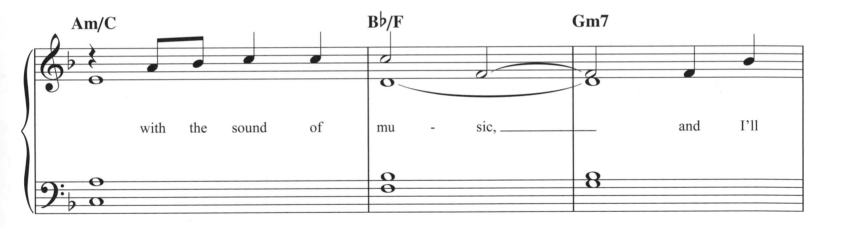

with the sound of mu - sic, _____ and I'll

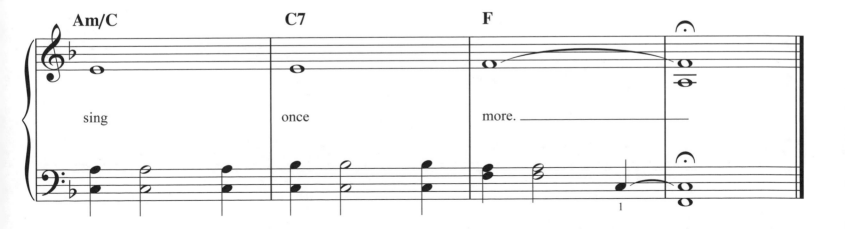

sing once more. _____

# TOMORROW

from the Musical Production ANNIE

Lyric by MARTIN CHARNIN
Music by CHARLES STROUSE

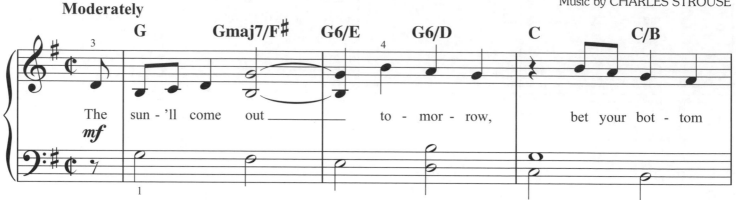

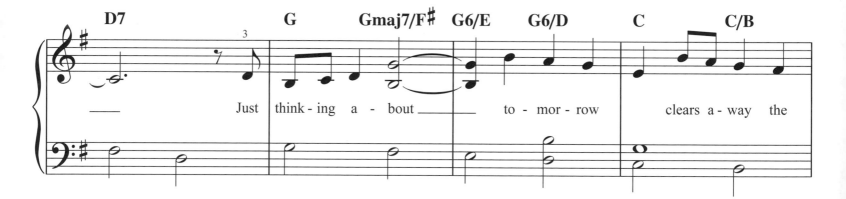

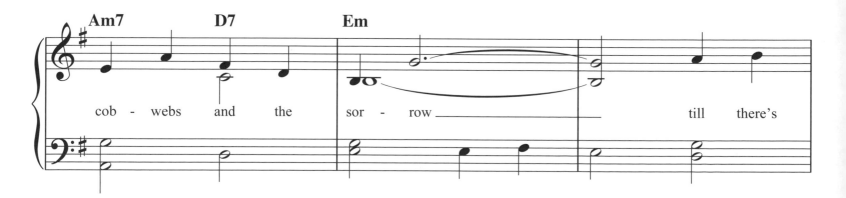

none. _____ When I'm stuck with a day that's

gray and lone - ly, _____ I just stick out my chin and

grin and say:

Oh, the sun - 'll come out _____ to - mor - row,

**C**         **Am7**   **D7**      **Em**

so you got to   hang on till to - mor - row, _____

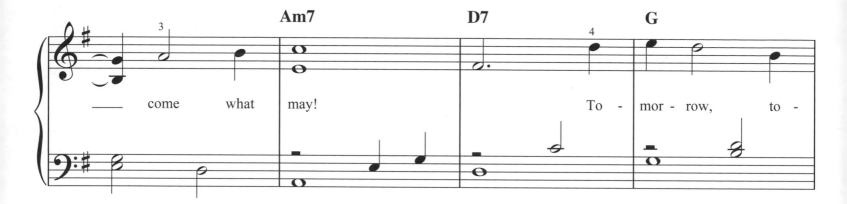

**Am7**        **D7**        **G**

___ come what may!       To - mor - row,   to -

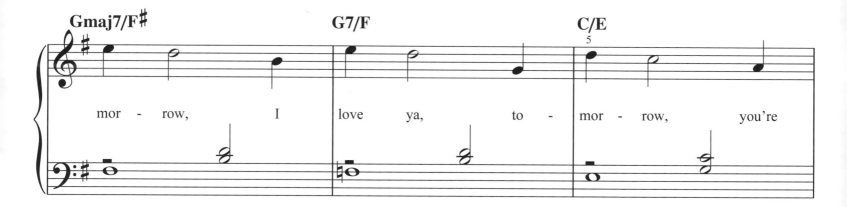

**Gmaj7/F♯**       **G7/F**       **C/E**

mor - row,   I   love ya,   to - mor - row,   you're

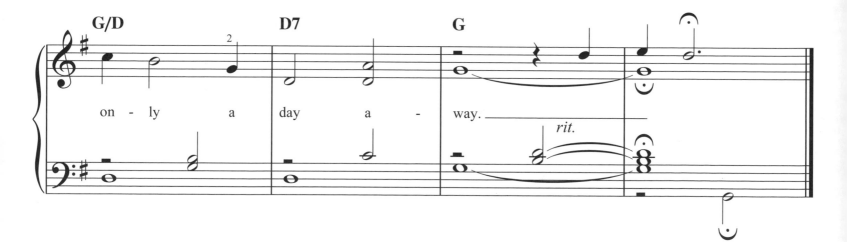

**G/D**       **D7**       **G**

on - ly a   day a -   way. _____

*rit.*

# WHERE IS LOVE?
## from the Broadway Musical OLIVER!

Words and Music by
LIONEL BART

74

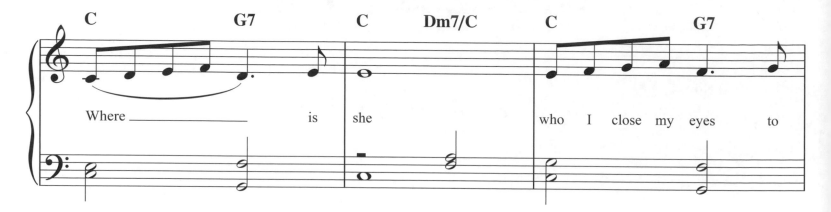

C   G7   C   Dm7/C   C   G7

Where _____ is she who I close my eyes to

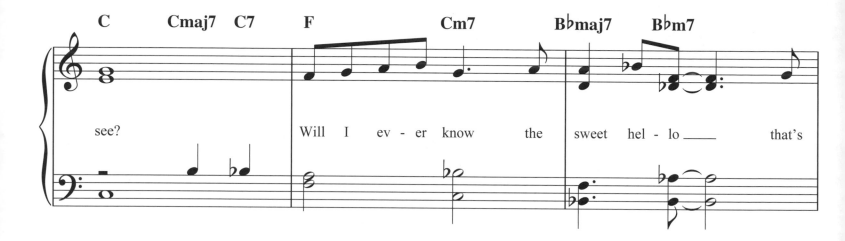

C   Cmaj7   C7   F   Cm7   B♭maj7   B♭m7

see? Will I ev - er know the sweet hel - lo _____ that's

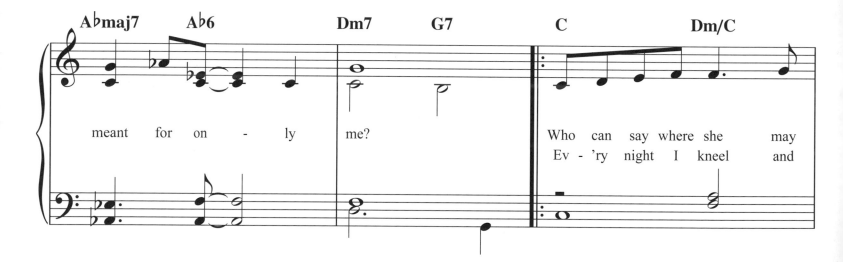

A♭maj7   A♭6   Dm7   G7   C   Dm/C

meant for on - ly me?

Who can say where she may
Ev - 'ry night I kneel and

C7   F   G7/F   Em   C#dim7

hide? Must I trav - el far and wide
pray, let to - mor - row be the day

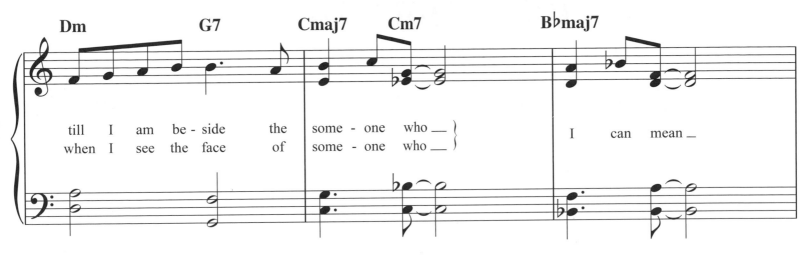

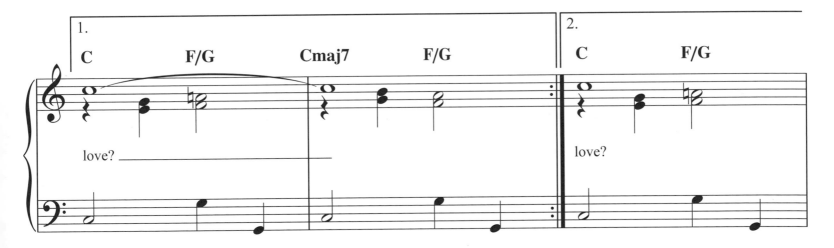

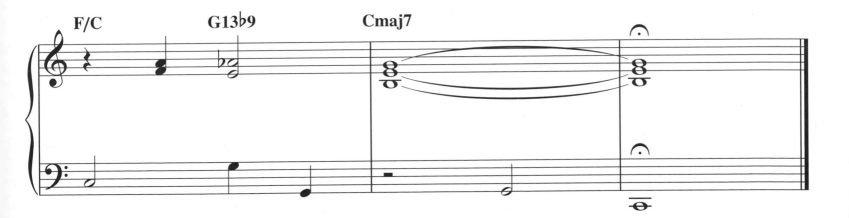

# WHO WILL BUY?

## from the Broadway Musical OLIVER!

Words and Music by
LIONEL BART

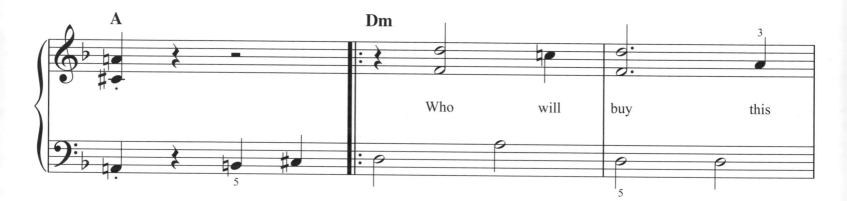

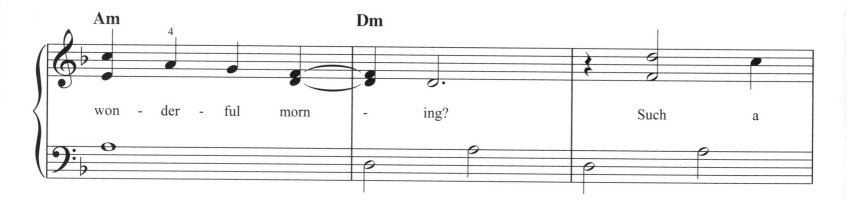

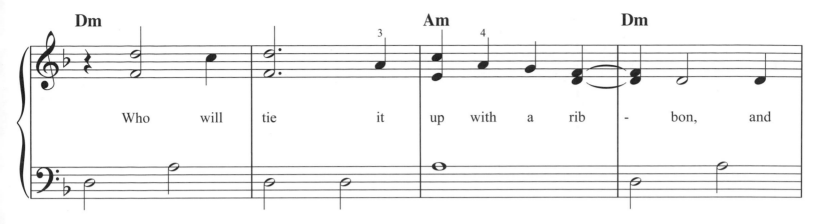

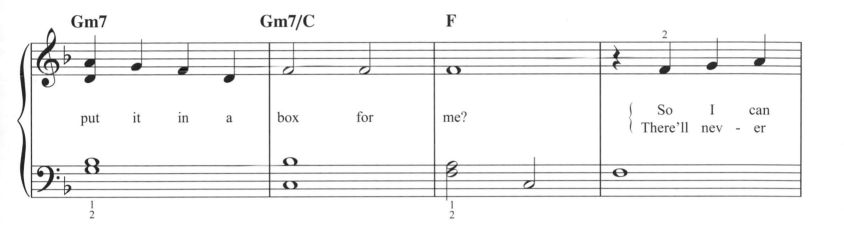

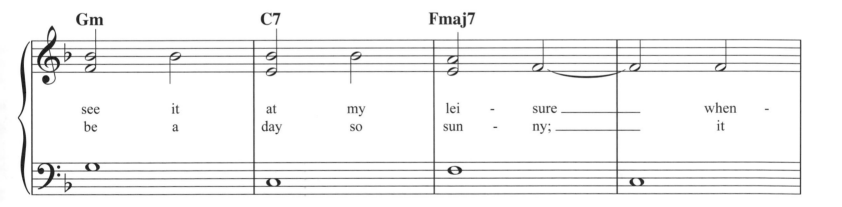

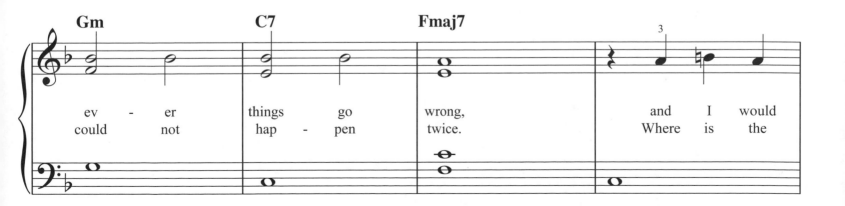

78

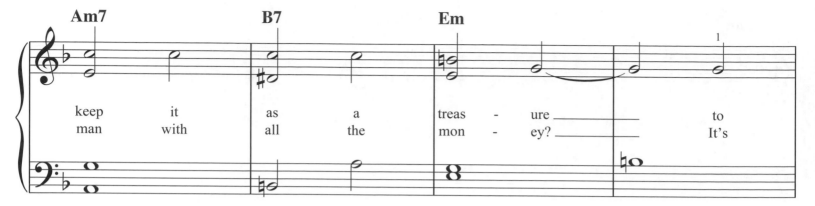

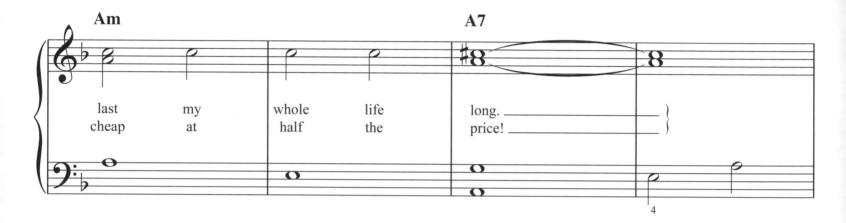

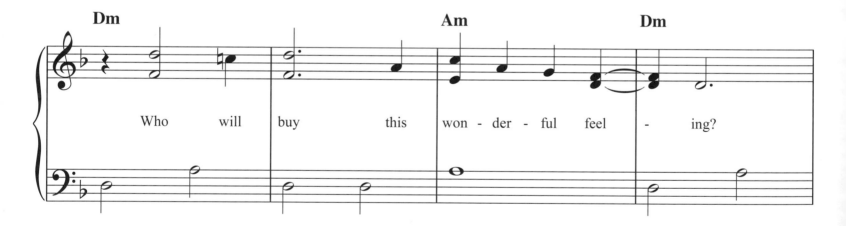

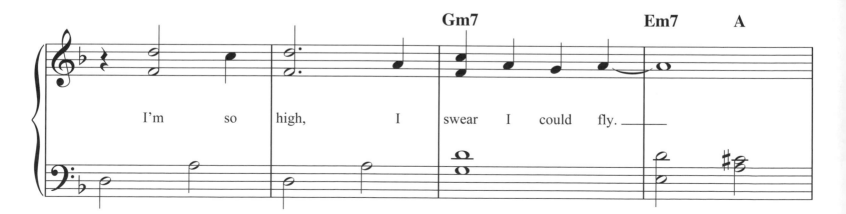

Me, oh, my, I don't want to lose _____ it, so

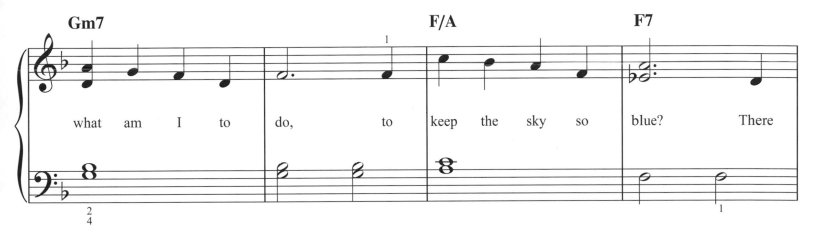

what am I to do, to keep the sky so blue? There

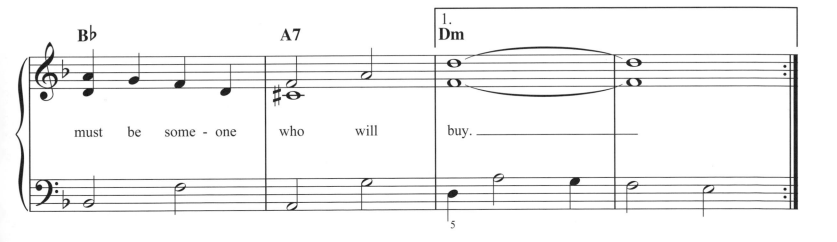

must be some - one who will buy. _____

buy.

# It's Easy to Play Your Favorite Songs with Hal Leonard Easy Piano Books

### Beatles Best for Easy Piano

Easy arrangements of 120 Beatles hits. A truly remarkable collection including: All My Loving • And I Love Her • Come Together • Eleanor Rigby • Get Back • Help! • Hey Jude • I Want to Hold Your Hand • Let It Be •
Michelle • many, many more.
00364092.........................................$24.99

### The Best Broadway Songs Ever

This bestseller features 80+ Broadway faves: All I Ask of You • I Wanna Be a Producer • Just in Time • My Funny Valentine • On My Own • Seasons of Love • The Sound of Music • Tomorrow • Younger
Than Springtime • more!
00300178 ............................................ $21.99

### The Best Praise & Worship Songs Ever

The name says it all: over 70 of the best P&W songs today. Titles include: Awesome God • Blessed Be Your Name • Come, Now Is the Time to Worship • Days of Elijah • Here I Am to Worship •
Open the Eyes of My Heart • Shout to the Lord • We Fall Down • and more.
00311312.........................................$19.99

### The Best Songs Ever

Over 70 all-time favorite songs, including: All I Ask of You • Body and Soul • Call Me Irresponsible • Edelweiss • Fly Me to the Moon • The Girl from Ipanema • Here's That Rainy Day • Imagine • Let It Be • Moonlight in
Vermont • People • Somewhere Out There • Tears in Heaven • Unforgettable • The Way We Were • and more.
00359223........................................$19.95

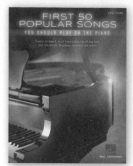

### First 50 Popular Songs You Should Play on the Piano

50 great pop classics for beginning pianists to learn, including: Candle in the Wind • Chopsticks • Don't Know Why • Hallelujah • Happy Birthday to You • Heart and Soul • I Walk
the Line • Just the Way You Are • Let It Be • Let It Go • Over the Rainbow • Piano Man • and many more.
00131140........................................$16.99

### Jumbo Easy Piano Songbook

200 classical favorites, folk songs and jazz standards. Includes: Amazing Grace • Beale Street Blues • Bridal Chorus • Buffalo Gals • Canon in D • Cielito Lindo • Danny Boy • The Entertainer • Für Elise •
Greensleeves • Jamaica Farewell • Marianne • Molly Malone • Ode to Joy • Peg O' My Heart • Rockin' Robin • Yankee Doodle • dozens more!
00311014.......................................$19.99

### Best Children's Songs Ever – 2nd Edition

This amazing collection features 101 songs, including: Beauty and the Beast • Do-Re-Mi • Hakuna Matata • Happy Birthday to You • If I Only Had a Brain • Let It Go • On Top of Spaghetti •
Over the Rainbow • Puff the Magic Dragon • Rubber Duckie • Winnie the Pooh • and many more.
00159272 Easy Piano....................................$19.99

### 150 of the Most Beautiful Songs Ever

Easy arrangements of 150 of the most popular songs of our time. Includes: Bewitched • Fly Me to the Moon • How Deep Is Your Love • My Funny Valentine • Some Enchanted Evening •
Tears in Heaven • Till There Was You • Yesterday • You Are So Beautiful • and more. 550 pages of great music!
00311316...............................................$24.95

### 50 Easy Classical Themes

Easy arrangements of 50 classical tunes representing more than 30 composers, including: Bach, Beethoven, Chopin, Debussy, Dvorak, Handel, Haydn, Liszt, Mozart, Mussorgsky, Puccini, Rossini, Schubert, Strauss,
Tchaikovsky, Vivaldi, and more.
00311215.........................................$14.99

### Today's Country Hits

A collection of 13 contemporary country favorites, including: Bless the Broken Road • Jesus Take the Wheel • Summertime • Tonight I Wanna Cry • When I Get Where I'm Goin' • When the Stars Go Blue • and more.
00290188.........................................$12.95

### VH1's 100 Greatest Songs of Rock and Roll

The results from the VH1 show that featured the 100 greatest rock and roll songs of all time are here in this awesome collection! Songs include: Born to Run • Good Vibrations • Hey
Jude • Hotel California • Imagine • Light My Fire • Like a Rolling Stone • Respect • and more.
00311110........................................$27.95

### Disney's My First Song Book

16 favorite songs to sing and play. Every page is beautifully illustrated with full-color art from Disney features. Songs include: Beauty and the Beast • Bibbidi-Bobbidi-Boo • Circle of Life • Cruella De Vil • A
Dream Is a Wish Your Heart Makes • Hakuna Matata • Under the Sea • Winnie the Pooh • You've Got a Friend in Me • and more.
00310322.........................................$16.99

Get complete song lists and more at **www.halleonard.com**
*Prices, contents, and availability subject to change without notice*

Disney characters and artwork © Disney Enterprises, Inc.

1216